A Sunken Ship

Written by Hawys Morgan

Collins

We sink.

The chill is a shock.

3

This shell is shut.

4

big shell

This fish is long.

wing fins

Shall we visit the ship?

Yes!

The dogfish is in the ship.

It zigzags.

11

We push up.

That was fun!

14

/nk/

15

After reading

Letters and Sounds: Phase 3

Word count: 39

Focus phonemes: /nk/ /sh/ /ch/ /ng/ /th/ /z/ /y/ /v/ /w/

Common exception words: we, the, push, was

Curriculum links: Understanding the World: The World

Early learning goals: Reading: use phonic knowledge to decode regular words and read them aloud accurately; demonstrate understanding when talking with others about what they have read

Developing fluency

- Your child may enjoy hearing you read the book.
- Take turns to read pages of the book with your child.

Phonic practice

- Ask your child:
  - Find and point to the /sh/ sound in these words: **ship**, **shock**, **fish**, **push**.
  - Which words have the /sh/ sound at the end and which words have the /sh/ sound at the beginning? (*/sh/ sound at the beginning: ship, shock; /sh/ sound at the end: fish, push*)
  - Can you think of any words that rhyme with **wing**? (e.g. *ring, bing, sing, thing, ding, ping, king*) These words all end in the /ng/ sound.
- Look at the "I spy sounds" pages (14–15) in the book. Discuss the picture with your child. How many items can your child see in the picture that have the /sh/ sound or the /nk/ sound? (*shore, ship, fish, shark, shop, shirt, shorts, shoes, dish, brush, tank, drink, pink, ink*)

Extending vocabulary

- The shell in the book is **big**. How many other words can your child think of that mean **big**? (e.g. *huge, large, giant, enormous, massive, colossal, oversized*)
- The chill was a **shock**. How many other words can your child think of that mean **shock**? (e.g. *surprise, unexpected, astonishing, startling*) Can your child make a shocked face?
- Can your child think of words to describe the fish on pages 6 and 7? (e.g. *big, long, strong, powerful, beautiful, graceful, scary, flat*)